The Lioness's share

Jan Mi

For a score had to be settled between God and self.

©Jan Mi May 2023

All rights reserved. No part of the publication may be copied, reproduced, distributed, or transmitted in any form by any means, including photocopying, recording to other electronic methods without the prior written permission of the author, except in the case of brief quotations embodied in reviews and certain non-commercial uses permitted by copyright law.

ISBN; 978-1-7394134-0-8

First published by kindle Direct publishing 2023

Layout: Jan Mi
Chapter Illustrations: Sonia Sonia

INTRODUCTION

Life throws many things in the works. Blood, flesh and bones; Pain, pleasure and a lot of in-betweens. Life is complex, success can be imperfect, and messy. Solutions aren't linear and answers may not be in plain sight. Adulting teaches us that. Life is understood backwards as you experience it.

The proceeding pages are a collection of prose and in their simplest form the author's inner thoughts and expressions of the lived experiences during her navigation of adulthood and search for meaning and purpose.
She explores at times conflicting sentiments through the lenses of Love and 'otherness' as well as God and spirituality.

Naked: stripped bare, masks off. The delivery is raw. The reader is absolutely entitled to their opinion and feelings on the issues- As is the author. she leaves these passages open for the interpretation of the reader.

The hope is that you enjoy this ride. May you be stirred to ask more questions, re-evaluate some social norms, back yourself more, fight for your place, be kind to yourself a little more and embody the lioness' spirit of bravery and courage through this jungle of life.

THE LIONESS

The hunter for the pride
A practical hustling ability in her arsenal
Innately strong, powerful, fierce
She has unmistakable speed
But she moves quietly.
And to her tactics many fall prey.

Although she sits at the top
of the food chain
It is a hard life
of being in constant battle
fighting for her territory.

But above all
She is commanding of respect
Worthy of attention
And has courage

For my inner circle.

TABLE OF CONTENTS

BONES

Slippery creatures	3
Up &down	4
The Lioness' share	5
Terminal	6
Shades of love	10
Lil Flower	11
knowing	12
Your shame	13
A love story	14
Love and hate	16
Not staying	17
The good	18
Denial	19
Effort	20
Shut it	21
Seriously though	22
Wild hearts	23
Juvenile	24
Seasons-Dear Jan	25

BLOOD

A day for the owner	28
Preparation	29
The unexpected	30
The clock ticks	31

In bloom	32
Green grass on the other side	33
The good	34
Home	35
Twisted	36
Animal instincts	37
Animal lovers	38
Breaking the ice	39
Indifference	40
The stage	41
chameleon	42
The door	43
One shitty job	44
The cage	45
Try again	46
Seeking knowledge	47
A moment	48
Psychological war fare	49
The irony	50
Betrayal	51
Other	52
Forgiving	53
Masks	54
All you have	55

FLESH

The hunt	*58*
Dare to dream	*59*

One man's meat	*60*
Seeds and weeds	*61*
Uncertainty	*62*
Its complicated	*63*
Questions-no-answers	*64*
Prayer	*65*
Letter to god	*66*
God's response	*67*
Destiny	*69*
Mountains	*70*
The gamble	*71*
Pain	*72*
Sacrifice	*73*
The dark	*74*
Agony	*75*
Dear God	*76*
Would you know?	*77*
True value	*78*
Things just are	*79*
A lioness's share	*80*
Follow the dream	*81*
The cost	*82*
Equality	*83*
Tough times	*84*
Forgiveness	*85*
Contentment	*86*
The prayer	*87*
This Lioness	*88*
The brave	*89*

The promise	*90*
A gem	*91*
A perfect storm	*92*
Freedom	*93*
Do better	94
Help is not coming	95
Legacy	96
Jungle rules	97
The light	98

BONES

Jungle story; Slippery creatures

As they walked through the jungle,
The lioness pointed to a curled up creature
and said to her cub.

'Little cub
We are strong and we are feared
But in this jungle
Be most aware of those slippery slitherers
Curled up, they purport harmlessness.
And when you least expect it

BOOM- venom- Sudden death
BOOM - cut circulation -Broken bones -Agonising death. '

Up and down

It's going to be a bumpy ride.
Hold on tight.
It will be alright in the end

The Lioness's share

She wished she would wake up
And it had all been
A bad dream

On that day of all days
She wished that God was real
And that he was coming
To save her

One last time
Don't fail me now
Take away the despair
She prayed !

Terminal

T1
Redundant in many ways
Unwilling to take responsibility for his actions.
A chronic liar, empty promises
His word cannot be relied upon.
A matter of routine
He seems to have done this all too often.

T2
The Tall, handsome, crisp dressed one
Smells good, talks right,
an object to be desired.
A respectable job, oh they bow at his presence
He is self-aware, too careful with his choices
Delicate taste
oh but he likes to engage
outside of his perfect marriage.

T3
Average in many ways
looks, lifestyle and dressing
For that is as far as his paycheck will reach
Great goals and plans to make it
In this cruel unfair world.
But only in his dreams they will remain
And alas the process of making it
will drain the experience

T4

Fair looks, no money,
but a decent purpose in life.
With a politeness that can only be credited
to the humility of poverty.
He too lives in the illusion
Of finding true love
Blind to the reality that they come at a price
which he cannot afford.
They who too are chasing after their own kind
Their decency of high value
and reserved only for those who can afford to pay for it.

T5.
Young, handsome with eclectic style
Semi schooled by choice
negative bank balance at best.
money goes towards the important things in life-
current trendy wear!
The chief financier is the accomplished but frustrated
middle aged woman who excitedly landed
a young fit good-looking man.
Except he is not available at prime time
He must live his edgy life with his true love;
a girlfriend his age.

T6.
But Alas the boy who will make no effort.
Oblivious to his lapse in basic hygiene
He will insult the girl who
does not desire him back.
And make claim to the fact that its her loss-
she "missed out on a good thing"
He will find solace in his mothers
house where love never dies

T7
Behold the ultimate lover.
The 'social 'reject.
Ultimately non-good looking by worldly standards.
For which he will overcompensate.
At the beck and call of the girl
who chose him for his humility.
The dynamic will only change after he makes it in life.
 Looks awareness will seem to vanish with new money.
Respect now a far-off dream.
she had loved him with no money nor looks
Short term memory fully activated.

T8
How about the one who was arranged for me
A perfect match by both our parents
Based on their in- depth knowledge of the good morals of the families.
Perhaps we shall find true intimacy in years to come.
For I shall learn to love him with time they say.

T9
What about your one?

Shades of love

And for a while
I genuinely loved them both
Each for different reasons
And they both knew me
Each in a different way
That if sat at a table together
They would both find it difficult
To reconcile the person they each knew
As the same person.

But In the end
I went with the one with whom
the relationship had been tested.
The one with whom many of my secrets lay
Who was never afraid of my wild choices
The one for whom I wore no armour
One with whom it was imperfect, messy but real.

Lil flower

Lil flower
Must they own you?
Isn't it enough to admire
your beauty by the roadside
rather than have you
In their possession
Where you will die after a week

Knowing

I know who I seek
And what I want
Although I cannot put it in words
Oh my soul
I will know when I encounter you
your presence will be undeniable to my soul
and you too will know
That I'm your designated.

Your shame

Why am I the one
Who is ashamed
When you are the betrayer?

Because you love another
Does that make me
Not good enough?

Why do I entertain you
Even when I know
How this story ends?

A Love story

If love be measured by the amount
of pain you endure,
then she had truly loved.
Even though she can't say
that it was always reciprocated.

She had been thorough
and indiscriminate in love
but when it was over
It hurt with equal measure
to the extent she had loved.

She knew not what was more bruised.
The heart, the ego or her confidence.
Perhaps all 3.
Motivated by the fear of rejection.
She gave up on love.
'You will love again'. They said to her.
And try she did.

In the end,
It was not the lack of trust in others.
It was the lack of trust in herself
To protect her heart

But mostly she feared to inflict upon others
The agony that had been borne in her heart.

Love and hate

I hate you

for not having loved me enough to stay

I love you

for the person I grew into after you.

Not staying

Not for all the time already invested

Not for all the memories we share

Not for the fear of the unknown

I will not stay because it would be self-betrayal.

The good

I love you too
But every time you have to fight to defend
Who you chose to love
It will be an exhausting battle
That will chip away at us

I know because I have been
Battling your kind
For some time now

Denial

I was still shocked
even though I had seen it coming.

I had imagined
that time would make it better
or that there was something I could do.

Effort

That 1 second half smile you wear
That looks like it's hurting you

Yeah, don't bother
It looks awkward.
And makes me feel
As uncomfortable as you do

Am sorry that
There is something about me
That makes you feel
Like you have to wear that fake smile
When you meet me down the corridor

I promise you that
Good morning is enough.

Shut it

When I made time for you
You were busy
When I wanted you
You wanted someone else

Don't show up now
Now that I have learned
To live without your validation

Don't show up now
To tell me that you see me
When I was always there
In front of you
But you looked far ahead

Don't show up now
Emotional whirlwind
To wreck everything in my path

seriously though

Dear future husband
I hear these people say
They 'don't take life too seriously'
I hope you are the kind who does take it seriously.
I don't need a clown
So I don't need you to be funny
Nor do I place any responsibility on you
To make me laugh.

wild hearts

The chains didn't tame her
She flirted with the rules
Loved the unhinged bad boys
who lived dangerously
So they could come home
And tell her about the adventure.
Vicariously through them
Her wild heart lived.

Juvenile

I ran into a former class mate the other day
That I hadn't seen since school days
I remember disagreeing and fighting about things
Many now trivial in relation to my adult cares
Some I laugh about now
And others I don't even remember
But somehow, I got the inkling
she wanted to pick up
where we left off at 14!

Dear Jan

Recognise when THEY are seasonal.

When their purpose in your life has been served.

Own the lesson and

Let them go.

BLOOD

Jungle story; A Day for the owner

Cub: Mama the hyena stole from us
The lioness: He was probably hungry too.
And we can only eat as much as can fill our bellies

Cub: So that makes it okay?
The lioness: It certainly doesn't make it okay
But it's to his detriment.
For he knows no other way than to steal.
It will only feed him for a day,
And makes him predictable.
For when he needs more food,
what do you think he will do?

Cub: come back again?
The lioness: that's right honey.
And Mama will be here
Expecting him.

Dear Jan

Always prepare yourself for the unexpected when setting out for any journey.

The unexpected

When I thought
I had it figured out
Only for it to smack me in the face

When I had made plans but
soon realised that
no part of our lives is ever
really in our full control.

The clock ticks

If you won't have it
Then someone else will
If you want it
Make haste.

In bloom

Lil Flower
They know your full potential
And as you grow taller
And reach full bloom,
Their aim will be
To pluck you

Continue to reach
towards the sun anyway
BLOSSOM

Green grass on the other side

She had as much talent
Never wavered in determination

What did they do so right?
What separated her from them?
What colour is their blood?
What did they feed on in their mother's wombs?
What wind was blowing on the day they were born?

What prayers do they say?
Do they even pray?

Are they as happy as they seem?
Do they have it all together?

She didn't care
She just wanted what they had for once

The good

I had trusted myself
To know what was good
But when it was in-front of me
I let it go by

Home

A place where no one asks where the accent is from

A Place where nothing reminds me of what I cannot have

A place where everything and everyone is imperfectly perfect

A place where the love they have for me feels more than the one I have for myself

A place where I am at one with you.

Twisted

I am not without a brain
Your language is just foreign to me

I am not weird
Your fun stuff is just not to my taste

I am not controversial
You just don't like the truth

I am not arrogant
I just refuse the boundaries
you so badly want to place upon me

I am not lonely
Just because am alone

Jungle story; Animal instincts

The little cub observed humans on a safari and asked;

Little cub; what are those machines they carry
The lioness; Guns
Little cub; whatever for
The lioness; protection from the animals
Little cub: then why won't they come closer?

The lioness; They are afraid of the big cats
Because we are untamed and unpredictable.
Don't mind the charades of the humans
They are every bit the animals we are
The stalking, aggression & killer instincts.
And when it matters to them,
They will tear into each other
And prey on the weaker ones.
They know to fear us and keep their distance
Because they are aware of themselves.

Animal lovers

You know the ones that save dogs

Have undying love for cats

But will devour fellow humans

These ones I fear.

Breaking the ice

We were no friends
Yet they too curious
asked too many questions
Never realising that they
were not privy to the information
and I was not compelled to share
So the answer was never going to be an honest one.

Indifference

In this life you will encounter
Some creepy
Some evil
Human beings
Waste no time nor energy on these ones.
Not even kindness
Can save them from themselves.

The stage

Nothing about her words was spontaneous.
Her indirect responses well-rehearsed
And an intentional weapon
Often mistaken for lack of clarity.

Conversation neutral
lest she betrayed her true unpopular opinion.
A kind word for many a situation
But all she wanted to say was
kindly fuck off
and cope on.

Her silence premeditated
Oh the mental exhaustion!
of playing dumb
But she would go far with the stupid card
The egocentrics remained unthreatened.

They would say of her
"oh she's a lovely and agreeable person."

Insignificant if you ask her.

Tragic!

Chameleon

The role you play.
The parts you invent
Solely to make people like you

At what point do you lose yourself
And start to believe your own lies?
The point at which you don't remember
what is truly yours
And what was made up for the world?

And you did it for acceptance
Of people you dislike.

Integration
They called it.

The door

Quick ! The door
How did she get here?

Deception !

She disarmed you
By acting a fool
By making you overlook her
When you let your guard down
She went through the next door

One shitty job

That job that you now despise
For dog whistle politics
The micro and passive aggression
Where the merit of promotion is questionable
The race is lost
Before it begins

Taking orders sensible or not
Because someone said they are the rules.
The compulsion to fake smiles and laughs
At that unfunny boss who cracks jokes.

It once paid the bills lets be honest
And for a while that was enough
And all that mattered
But it now floods the soul

The cage

A prisoner in my own skin

Trapped by the high standards

To which I hold myself

And expectations

That I have for myself.

Dear Jan

When you find yourself on the losing side,

Remember that there is another chapter to be told.

Wake up and try again

Tomorrow will present another set of opportunities.

Jungle story; seeking knowledge

The Lioness observed while her little cub tirelessly made attempts to climb the tree and had gone over to her friend the pig for help. After futile attempts the cub returned to its mother frustrated.

The lioness: what's with the long face little cub .

The cub: piggy and I couldn't quite figure out how to climb the tree.

The Lioness: well, you should have gone over to the monkey instead of
　　　　　piggy.

The cub: But piggy is my friend.

The lioness: But piggy doesn't know how to climb trees.
And you have it in you, but piggy doesn't stand a chance. He will only hold you back with his fears.

A moment

We joked and laughed
For a moment I forgot.
We shared heartfelt stories
For a moment we were one.

Then your people came
Suddenly a deafening silence
Invisible I became
Our differences illuminated.

Without much being said
I was conscious of the fact
That I was lost
That this was not my tribe
And that I wasn't welcome.

And although you tried
In the battle for politeness
You lost the fight
You were outnumbered.

The battle was exhausting.
You gave up on me too!

Psychological war fare

Black history month; A time to celebrate the heroes and milestones
In the fight for equality.

Lets In essence remind the neutral folks
To take pity on the people of colour
Who need their sympathy and
understanding for being black

While we are at it
Remind black folks of their place in history
Once inferior servants
Who would have nothing if not
For the sympathy of the nice white folk
That developed a conscience
and joined their cause
After having transplanted them against their will.

And by God with the annual history celebration
Let's dedicate a day or month to this cause
Lest the new generation of white folks
are raised without the knowledge upon
which they must act
All but in revised skill.

Irony

She breaks bank to acquire

Features genetically typical of my kind

Full lips

Dark/tan skin

Ample bosom

Big bottom

Her definition of beauty

For which she strives

Yet she still thinks my tribe inferior.

Betrayal

Like a prompted pact

The room stayed silent

All of them having known the truth

But none brave enough to defend it

They watched her burn.

Other

When I didn't speak your language
I was marginalized.
when I learned it
With surprise you comment
On how good it is
As if it was never expected to be so

Are you afraid of me
now that I speak your language?
Or are you afraid
that now that I have measured up to your culture
I may find it wanting
And that it was represented better
than it is in reality

Forgiving

I forgive you
Not because you are deserving of it
I forgive you because
You are a flawed human like all others
Self-included

I forgive you because
I know nothing of your own suffering
And struggles

I forgive you for my own sake
That I may be free.

Masks

'I have a resting bitch face .' She said.
I silently agreed.

But she said it like it was something
to be proud of!

All you have

For all you have overcome

For all you have accomplished against the grain

For all you have set yourself up to BE.

You are a FORCE

FLESH

Jungle story 4. The hunt

As the pride was gathering for the hunt, the little cub asked her mum why they all had to go.

The Lioness; Because little one
Together we are a powerful force
If we hunt as a pride, a coalition
The game is up for the target
They can't outrun us
And we won't be out muscled
we have more efficiency and strength in numbers.

Dare to dream

What if it's possible

What if it's mine

One man's meat

The other day an acquaintance asked
How I would be spending my weekend.
At home watching something I said,
How sad, she said
'Do you want to come to church?'
All weekend? How sad I thought.
No I responded.

Seeds and weeds

They say that on the path of life
We plant seeds as we go along
Evidently some weeds tend to grow
alongside the good crop.

Did someone plant the weeds
Or do they grow on their own accord?

Why do they tend to choke
the good crop?

Who weeds them out?
Does he get ever get them?

Uncertainty

The existence of a higher power
I do not question

Of prayer and its power
I remain in doubt

Its complicated

Sunny days, rainy days
Life doesn't promise us only the good

Pain and pleasure
Bad things happen
To good people too

seasons change
We must wait
Before we reap

Questions-no answers

If things are not really as they appear
Then what is truth?

What are the limits
To our knowledge?

What are we missing?

Are the real answers in plain sight?

Is the road travelled by many a diversion?

Are we asking the right questions?

Prayer

My dear friends
that believe in prayer
Tell me please that
I may know the hacks
What words to use
that your god delivers
What language you speak
that catches his ear
Tell me the length of time
You must labour in prayer

Letters to God

Dear God
We are taught
That you are faithful.
That You are the beginning
And the end
That your will must be done
on earth as it is in heaven.

I ask myself
In time of suffering
Why God ?
if you are a loving father?
How have you willed this burden upon my life?

I ask myself
How those who don't bow to you
Have what I pray for.

I ask myself when I have done all in my power
 why you won't meet me half way

Oh dear God ,show your face
And settle this score.

God's response

Show my face Jan?
Do not be quick to forget
The times the odds were tipped in your favour

Remember those unanswered prayers
When I knew better
That what you prayed for
wasn't what was best for you
You sighed...Thank god . Dodged a bullet there.

Remember that closed door
When you thought the game was up
And I led you through a new GATE?

Coincidence- is there such a thing?
I sent you one too many.
In a conspiracy to get you here

What about the 3 talents bestowed upon you
Talents unused
Which would have you out of that job
That you very much despise.

Dear Jan
I have already met you half way
Quit mourning and whining
Get out there
And do what you know you have to do
Everything is already within your power!

GO!

Destiny

They said,

It was luck
It was coincidence
It was forces outside my control

That I was not the loss or failure
Nor was I the success or win

That no matter how little I did
Or how hard I worked
Destiny made the result so.

Mountains

The intentions had been good
But Mistakes were made
Soldier on Little warrior
Even though alone you must fight

The gamble

The risks taken
A coin toss
knowing that you
could potentially lose

You swing
You lose
But you know
It just as easily
Could have gone your way

Pain

when happily ever after
Isn't what it had promised to be.

Sacrifice

When the price of the dream
Turned out to be high

Immense loneliness.

The dark

When in spite of being at the center
of the matter,
you are the last to know.

Agony

The windy road ahead
when the path that you chose
Tests you .

Failure
Almost
So close
Not quite
No
Better luck next time!

Dear God

Have I believed to the point of being delusional?

If you truly exist,

it would be nice to hear from you for once.

And IF you do show up,

may it leave no room for doubt that it was you.

Dear Jan

Would you recognise me if I was in front of you

Would you recognise my voice if you heard it ?

Would you?

The fact that you have to question solidifies the doubt that you would.

I have showed up many a time

In big moments that appear little to you now

True Value

Oxygen- free for all

Talent- free at birth

blood & organs- donated

Love & friendship - given

Rainwater - free falling

Life.

....

True value was never bought.

Dear Jan

we don't always get to know why.

Some things just Are.

Jungle story; A lioness' share

The little cub was mourning to her mother about why they had to work hard for the day's food. She was obsessing about a sparrow that just had to fly.

Lioness: you see the sparrow,
its problem is insects and worms.

YOU are built for elephant problems.
Neither insects nor worms
will satisfy you.

You are built for the task.
 speed, brute strength, bravery, claws
 and sharp jaws to take down an elephant.

That is the lioness' share.

Dear Jan

Be clear in your mind what your dreams really are

Then Follow the dream.

The cost

She is in constant vibration

She strives for balance

Not stability

And sometimes

That Balance must be attained

At the cost of stability.

Equality

Dear Jan

From the outset all are born equal

All naked

All with the same 24hrs a day.

So what's your excuse?

Tough times

At the time it had seemed like a catastrophe

As time has passed,

It is but a tiny fragment

In the memory of my journey.

Forgiveness

I forgive myself
For holding back due to fear of rejection
For the scars I have unwittingly
Brought upon myself
Through poor choices
Through hesitation and indecision
Through misplaced love and trust

Contentment

I look at a throwback photo
From a few years ago
And I wish I could go back
To that time when I was happier
And then am reminded
That even in the time of the photo
I must have thought there was
A happier time in the past.
Must I understand happiness
backwards?

I look to the future
To when I have this
And achieved that
Happiness Still far ahead of me
And when I have achieved it all
It doesn't feel like I had imagined.

Is it ever present?
Are we Ever truly content
Would we stop if we were?

The prayer

Grant me the strength
To fulfil my life's purpose
Needing no one's approval but my own.
To do things for the right reasons
regardless of the consequences.
To reserve my trust for those who have earned it
Not to conform to standards outside of my values.
To dedicate time and energy towards my missions.
To always do my best.
And above all
Not just to survive through life
But to show up for it
And be present.

This Lioness

Thunder like roars
Deadly claws
And if you can't outrun her
She's going for the jugular.

The brave

It might not be open forever.
And you will never know what's behind it
If you don't go through that door.

The promise

The task was
To worry not

The promise was that
In the end
Everything will be okay

A gem

When this diamond
is finally polished
I will owe it to
The intense heat
The pressure
The storms
The wrecking balls
The volcanic eruptions
That thrust it to the surface
And most of all

TIME !

A perfect storm

And the storm
It wreaked havoc in its wake
A violent disturbance
Which we had to endure
If we wanted the rain
It brought with it.

Freedom

To be free from
The bondage of public opinion
The need to judge
The need to have an opinion
And Preserving things
like you will live forever

Do better

Better than the generation before
Better than they expected you to
Better than yesterday.

Bend if you have to
Rest and Flex if you must
But NEVER BREAK.

Help is not coming

She knew where she stood
Because she wasn't waiting on anyone
To come and save her

Legacy

Stubborn; she wouldn't be denied.
Determined; No matter what life threw at her
Contrary; she did it her way.

Jungle story; Jungle rules

As her little cub grew up. The lioness sat her down and said;
As I have lived, I have found there are certain rules that will serve you best
To remember.

1. There is a pecking order
2. Eat or be eaten
3. The jungle rewards those best suited to survive
4. Don't underestimate the animal that squares up to you.
5. If you grow big enough you can make up the rules

The light

It got hard before it got easier

Darkness loomed for a long time

For what seemed like eternity

But in the end light prevailed.

In the end my dreams were bigger than my fear

THE END

Thank you for having read this far.

I went with my heart on whatever I wrote about. Am glad it resonated with you enough for you to stick with it until the end.

Kindly consider leaving a review.

CONNECT

Instagram ; @jan_mi_jm

TikTok: @jan.mi_

www.ingramcontent.com/pod-product-compliance
Lightning Source LLC
Chambersburg PA
CBHW061450040426
42450CB00007B/1291